NOURISHING LITTLE LIVES

50 RECIPES THAT WILL HELP YOUR MINI THRIVE

BY DANNI DUNCAN

Copyright @ Danielle Duncan
Published by Ingram
Photography by Michelle Bolitho
Design by Helena Berggren

ISBN: 978-0-6454738-1-0
Hardback Edition

All rights reserved. The moral right of the author has been asserted. No part of this book may be reproduced in any mechanical, photographic or electronic process; nor may it be stored in a retrieval system, transmitted or otherwise be copied for public or private use, without written permission from the author. You must not circulate this book in any format.

This publication contains the opinions and ideas of the author. It is intended to provide helpful and informative material on the subjects addressed. While the author has used their best efforts in preparing this publication, the material is of the nature of general comment only. Any use of information in this book is at the reader's discretion and risk. The author can not be held responsible for any loss, claim or damage arising out of the use, or misuse, of any suggestions made, or for any material on third party websites.

The information provided within this book is general in nature and is not intended as personal nutrition and food advice. For personal advice consult your dietitian or medical professional.

CONTENTS

INTRODUCTION	1
DANNI'S TOP TIPS	7-9
PART 1: THE INFO	10
- WHEN TO INTRODUCE	10
- BREASTFEEDING	13
- NUTRIENTS AND KEY VITAMINS	14-15
- ROUTINE AND ALLERGENS	16-17
- GAGGING AND CHOKING	18
- FOOD CHOICES	20
PART 2: THE RECIPES	22
- FIRST TASTES	22
- 6 MONTHS+	25
- 9 MONTHS+	67
PART 3: GROWING UP	95
- 12 MONTHS AND TODDLERS	96
HOW TO COOK	126-129
REFERENCES AND FURTHER READING	132
ABOUT THE AUTHOR	133
INDEX	142

INTRODUCTION

WELCOME TO THE FUN, MESSY AND SOMETIMES CHALLENGING MILESTONE THAT IS INTRODUCING SOLIDS.

It's a journey, for sure, and every single one is different and unique. There will be days when your baby loves one thing and they throw it the next. There will be frustration, a lot of mess, smiles and no doubt, tears. It will take trial and error, persistence, patience and resilience.

This is an area of motherhood I love for so many reasons. My husband, Chris, and I are both huge lovers of food, for nutritional reasons but also for enjoyment. Ensuring our kids have the same love was important for us. Not only so we can enjoy family meals together, but knowing that our kids are fueling their bodies well means one less thing we have to worry about as parents. I have been wanting to write this book for 3 years and I'm so excited that it is finally here.

It is so important for our children to get all of their nutrients. Creating good eating habits from the start is the first step in making sure this happens. Ensuring our kids get all of their vitamins and minerals is vital for the development of all their cells, including brain function, organ function, bone strength, and energy production. Not only this but getting our kids to eat a variety of food, and enjoy nutrient dense food, creates great habits for the future and ensures a positive and healthy relationship with food as they grow.

So here is a little secret… even though this area is my jam, we had a terrible start with our first born, Harper. I had zero clue about where to start. At around four months she was showing signs of interest: reaching for my food and eyeing it off, so we decided to give it a go. Rice cereal seemed like the right place to start - it wasn't. Within two weeks of starting Harper on solids we had a trip booked, to Bali, so I stocked up on loads of pre-made pouches which are jam packed with fruit. Once we got back from our twelve day holiday I figured I should try and give her some more vegetables by themselves and she flat out refused. It was then I decided to do more research and we re-started our journey.

For me, I only want good, high quality food going into my kids' bellies to ensure that they have the best chance to thrive and grow, to be as healthy as possible and educated around what their bodies need. If I won't eat it, I won't feed it to my kids! This includes things that I see so many parents give their kids which is commonly thought to be ok. It is important to remember that foods including ham, pre packaged snacks, sweets and fast food are all enjoyable foods in moderation, however, in my house we call these "sometimes foods". Research shows that high consumption of some of these foods increases the risk of certain cancers, obesity and diabetes and are not good for long term health.

I want you to remember that each child is different. I know this because all of my kids have been different - even the twins. Beau took to food at 4.5 months like he was in heaven and ate everything and anything like a champion. Although he feeds himself and eats with his hands, Beau liked to be spoon fed and waited on. Harlow on the other hand took a bit longer to start enjoying solids. She started around the 7 month mark and loved to feed herself. Harlow is also very stubborn and if she didn't want something, she definitely let us know. This is where my persistence and patience come into play. Ensuring you are allowing kids to be individuals will help them develop in their own ways. Try not to compare your baby to anyone elses and if you do hit a roadblock or are concerned, bring it up with your doctor, your maternal health nurse or a childhood nutritionist to get some direction.

Even though I am a Nutrition Coach, I am not qualified in the baby/child space which is why I have teamed up with the beautiful Courtney Bates from Healthy Bods Nutrition as a contributor to this book. Courtney is an accredited dietitian and nutritionist with a special interest in child nutrition. She and I have similar values when it comes to nourishing ourselves and our kids. Courtney is a mum of two and loves helping parents in this space. I love learning and educating myself on all areas of life, so I have loved working with her on this book.

I hope this book gives you the confidence and guidance you need to create your own good little eater. So that you can enjoy family meals together, ensure your child has a great relationship with food from day dot, and has everything they need to thrive. **I hope you love this process as much as me. Happy cooking (and feeding).**

LOVE AND LIFE
DANNI, CHRIS, HARPER, HARLOW & BEAU X

A NOTE FROM COURTNEY FROM HEALTHY BODS NUTRITION

The definition of weaning is *the transition of babies from breast or formula milk to nourishment with solids. It begins with the first mouthful of solids and ends with the last breast or formula milk feed.*

Starting solids with your baby is such an exciting milestone! It is important to provide your baby with adequate nutrients like iron which starts to deplete at around 6 months. Research has shown good nutrition in the first 1,000 days (the moment of conception until a child turns 2), can lay down the foundations for a lifetime of health. Virginia Woolf said it best, "One cannot think well, love well, sleep well, if one has not dined well."

Learning to eat requires the use of all eight senses - sight, taste, touch, sound, smell, vestibular (balance), proprioceptive (movement) and interoceptive (internal).
So, it is not an easy task to learn to do!

DANNI'S TOP TIPS

CREATING NON FUSSY EATERS FROM DAY 1

1. Babies aren't born disliking food. They have no idea if they like something or not. When we first start introducing foods it can take anywhere between 10 and 15 times for them to accept a texture and flavour. Food refusal does not mean that they don't like it. It could mean a variety of things: they're not sure, they're not hungry, or that they are still getting used to that texture or flavour. It's super important not to force food on babies as this could result in them having a negative association with that food. Popping it on the plate consistently means they have the opportunity to always try it.

2. It's so common when our babies don't eat what we've given them to offer something else that they like. This 'something else' is usually something sweet like fruit. I mean we want them to eat, right? My tip around this is to try to avoid giving an alternative. By giving them something else, when they refuse what you've offered, means that in the future they will repeat the same behaviour and they'll never learn to eat and like the food you've offered. The difficulty also leads to parents making multiple meals just to get their kids to eat. In my house, if you don't eat what I've put in front of you, you go to bed hungry. Sounds harsh I know - but if they're hungry, they will eat. Try not to panic!

3. When introducing solids, like with the above tip, sometimes we do whatever is "easiest" for the sake of the now. The problem here is that it turns into "far too often." Whether it is offering something sweet to just get them to eat, or fatty or fast food, it's not a good long term solution. I want you to think beyond the now and think of the future, the habits you're creating for them and the nutrients for their growing bodies. (Ensuring you have a lot of prepped foods will help.)

4. I know it can be scary and daunting offering bigger pieces of food, and a lot of parents I speak to are scared that their baby will choke but try to not let your fears hold back your child's development. Educate yourself on what to do if your baby does choke but know that gagging is a great skill for them to learn as they push the food forward rather than swallowing something that is too big. Chances are your fears won't come to fruition and not allowing your baby to have finger food or bigger textures is holding them back from learning new skills. (More on gagging and choking on page 16.)

5. One thing I see so many parents do is have never ending snacks and unfortunately they're not always good ones. It is important to try and avoid creating a snacking habit. Not only does this mean they're probably not eating their full meals at meal times, which then leads to frustration for you, but a lot of snacking means your baby or toddler isn't experiencing hunger or satiety which are really important. Knowing when you're hungry and when you're full helps you as you get older as studies have found that snacking in childhood can lead to obesity.

6. Exposure, exposure exposure! I can't reiterate this enough. The moment that you stop offering a food because you think your child doesn't like it is the moment that you stop giving them the opportunity to explore that flavour over and over again. They don't have to always eat it - but keep offering it to them.

7. We want our children to not only be nourished by the food that we give them but also to feel full - especially before bed. Making sure they have adequate protein in their diet (around 14g a day for babies 7-12 months and 14g for toddlers 1-3 years[6]) means that they will be fuller for longer. In turn helping them to sleep for longer stints and providing the essential nutrients to grow their muscles and bones.

8. There will be times when your child just doesn't want to eat. Forcing them to eat is not recommended as there could be various reasons as to why. Are they hungry? Sick? Or even teething. If you have waited a good period of time between milk and solids and your baby just isn't interested, remove the child from the environment, and do a restart 15-30 minutes later. When children are sick or teething, their appetite will go down - just like you or me. So, try not to stress!

9. We can't expect our children to eat a variety of foods and flavours if we won't, so role modelling for your kids is super important. Try to have some meals together, eating the same foods - showing them and leading by example as to how much you enjoy them. This worked so well for Harper as she grew into toddler hood and became more aware. If Mummy and Daddy were eating it, she would want to as well. Being able to sit down and have family meals together without worrying what to feed the kids also makes it much easier later on.

10. My 6 P's. Prior Preparation Prevents Piss Poor Performance. Ok, so, basically, prep as much as you can! All of my recipes can be prepped and frozen, no matter if it's lunch or dinner, if you're running late or just can't be bothered cooking, you always have something to nourish your child. Most of my recipes won't take long, so set some time aside and get cooking. If you have twins - I feel you - prepping double the amount of food is a lot - but it will help you so much.

11. This is another one around fear - the fear of an allergy. Try not to let this put you off introducing your baby to foods early on. Know the signs, watch for them and educate yourself on what to do. But, at the end of the day, it needs to be done. (Keep reading for tips around allergens.)

12. Enjoy the process of introducing solids. Try not to stress too much. It's a journey and the more calm you can be the more fun it'll be for all the parties involved. Get creative, let them explore different textures, flavours, spices and cuisines. Take photos, take videos of the process as they are cheeky and you can get some great pictures of them in their messy states. Remember mess is a part of it! Try and let go of your need for a clean space and let them get their hands in there. My babies have always loved using their hands. Getting used to textures is great for their sensory development and coordination. Get some good cloths and be prepared to do a lot of cleaning up!

> **DID YOU KNOW IT CAN TAKE 10-15 EXPOSURES OF A FOOD FOR IT TO BE ACCEPTED?**

PART 1

WHEN TO INTRODUCE:

The Australian Infant Feeding Guidelines recommend commencing solids from six months of age. At this stage infants are physiologically and developmentally ready for new foods, textures and modes of feeding and need more nutrients than what breast milk or formula provide.[3]

In saying that, some babies show signs of readiness before this. From four months old babies can be developmentally ready. If you are finding your baby showing signs, you are able to commence solids earlier but always consult your doctor or maternal health nurse if you're unsure.

REMEMBER EACH BABY IS DIFFERENT, AND SOME MAY TAKE LONGER THAN OTHERS.

SIGNS OF READINESS INCLUDE:

✓ THEY ARE ABLE TO SIT IN A HIGH CHAIR AND SUPPORT THEIR NECK

✓ THEY ARE INTENTIONALLY REACHING FOR FOOD.

✓ THEY WATCH FOOD WITH INTEREST.

✓ THEY HOLD THEIR MOUTHS OPEN AS IF THEY ARE TRYING TO GET

SIGNS THEY MAY NOT BE READY:

✗ THEY PUSH ANY FOOD OUT AND FORWARD WITH THEIR TONGUE (TONGUE THRUST).

✗ THEY CAN'T SUPPORT THEIR HEAD.

MILK

The World Health Organization (WHO) recommends that "infants are exclusively breastfed until around 6 months of age when solid foods are introduced, and that breastfeeding is continued until 12 months of age and beyond, for as long as the mother and child desire."[4]

Breastmilk contains carbohydrates, proteins, fats and fluid. In addition, it contains factors including antibodies, white blood cells and human milk oligosaccharides (HMOs) which can help protect against infection and contribute to a child's immune system and healthy gut microbiome. HMOs act as prebiotics, feeding the good bacteria in your baby's gut.

Although breastmilk is the best nutritional choice for babies, breastfeeding is not always possible for so many reasons which is why fed is best. Formula is a breastmilk substitute often made from cow's milk which provides babies with the nutrients they need to grow. Other types of formulas include soy based formulas, pre-digested formulas and hypoallergenic formulas.

TIP! TRY NOT TO WIPE YOUR BABY'S MOUTH BETWEEN MOUTHFULS AS THIS CAN CREATE A NEGATIVE ASSOCIATION WITH MEALTIMES AND POSSIBLE FUSSINESS.

MY BREASTFEEDING JOURNEY

I had always intended to breastfeed Harper and after a few latching issues in the first instance, we started off really well and I had a good supply. However, as the weeks went on a combination of my impatience, Harper's reflux, stress and a lack of sleep - my supply seemed to drop quite significantly and a trip to the maternal health nurse at four months showed she hadn't put on the amount of weight she should've for her age. This added stress didn't help my milk supply and I was encouraged to start including a formula feed once a day. Although I loved the closeness breastfeeding brought at certain times, I didn't love my body, I didn't love the hassle and eventually over the next two months we slowly started to drop feeds. I had massive guilt around choosing to stop breastfeeding at six months but in the end it was the best thing for our family. I was a happier mum and Harper was still a happy baby.

The twins' journey was also interesting. After what I thought wasn't the most successful journey with Harper, the thought of breastfeeding the twins scared me and made me anxious. I didn't want to commit either way but we got my pump ready in case I decided to go ahead and try. The fact that they both ended up in special care and I was unable to hold them initially motivated me so much to try and do whatever I could for them. I pumped around the clock to give them whatever I could. The first few weeks, although tiresome, were amazing. I produced so much milk for my little darlings. Once strong enough, I would put each of them on my boob at some stage during the day too, which I really loved. That closeness is so nice. However again, at around six weeks I was so exhausted from pumping every four hours while looking after twins and a toddler, I decided to stop pumping, with over 8 litres of frozen milk. I was so proud of what I had achieved when I thought I wouldn't do it at all.

At the end of the day, fed is best and the fact that I was able to give my little loves even a little breast milk was an achievement. As mothers we put too much pressure on ourselves. The guilt around swapping to formula can be intense. I felt this, but, as we moved through the journey I realised as long as they were nourished it didn't matter.

NUTRIENTS AND KEY VITAMINS

FOOD BEFORE 1 IS NOT JUST FOR FUN

I'm sure you've all heard the phrase, "food before 1 is just for fun." Unfortunately, this is outdated and quite frankly just not true. I know when you're feeling stressed that it can reassure you that it's not important. However, in addition to being fun, food is essential for sensory development, social interactions and nutrition.

Ensuring your baby has a variety of foods means that you're giving your baby enough nutrients for them to grow and thrive in their infancy. They are growing so quickly it's important that they get a range of nutrients from a range of sources.

Once you have done your first tastes and your baby is accepting foods more easily, it's important to offer variety. Just like adults, ensuring that your baby is getting food from each of the five food groups can ensure that they are getting all of their nutrients. I have listed the food groups below as advised by Eat for Health - The Australian Guide to Healthy Eating and a list of the key nutrients that our babies need when starting solids.[5]

THE 5 FOOD GROUPS:

VEGETABLES AND LEGUMES/BEANS

MILK, YOGHURT CHEESE AND/OR ALTERNATIVES, MOSTLY REDUCED FAT

LEAN MEATS AND POULTRY, FISH, EGGS, TOFU, NUTS AND SEEDS

FRUIT

GRAIN (CEREAL) FOODS, MOSTLY WHOLEGRAIN AND/OR HIGH CEREAL FIBRE VARIETIES

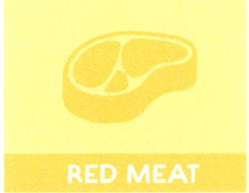    

| RED MEAT | BEANS | NUTS | SPINACH | IRON |

| OILY FISH (SALMON) | OMEGA 3 |

KEY NUTRIENTS

| LEGUMES | POULTRY | EGGS | SOY PRODUCTS | ZINC |

| YOGHURT | CHEESE | MILK | CALCIUM |

| FISH | CHICKEN | EGGS | IODINE |

| WHOLE GRAIN | BEANS | FRUIT | VEGETABLES | FIBRE |

THE ABOVE ARE A FEW EXAMPLES OF WHERE YOU WILL FIND THESE NUTRIENTS.

ROUTINE

My family has always started by introducing solids at lunch time. (This way if they were to have any reaction then there is time afterwards to watch for signs.) It is important to leave enough time between your baby's milk feed and solids to ensure they are actually hungry for food. Imagine getting a plate of food put in front of you after a big glass of milk and being told to eat - you'd probably push it away too.

From around 6.5 months, when the babies started eating 3 meals a day, until 10 months, we offered milk first, then solids 1.5 hours later. Our routine looked something like this:

7:00AM WAKE - MILK FEED
8:30AM - BREAKFAST
9:00AM - NAP

11:30AM WAKE - MILK FEED
1:00PM - LUNCH
1:30PM - NAP

4:00PM WAKE - MILK FEED
5:30PM - DINNER
7:00 MILK FEED AND BED

6 MONTHS

At 10 months we swapped to offering breakfast first and dropped a bottle - our routine then looked like this:

7:00 - WAKE AND BREAKFAST
8:30AM - MILK FEED
9:30AM - SNACK
10:00AM-1030AM NAP

12:00PM WAKE
12:30PM LUNCH
2:00PM MILK FEED
3:00PM-3:30PM NAP

4:00PM WAKE
4:30PM-5:00PM DINNER
7:00PM MILK FEED AND BED

10 MONTHS

At around 11.5 months we then started to introduce a cows milk bottle instead of a formula bottle so that when they turned one they were solely on cows milk. At 12 months we also dropped the afternoon bottle and introduced a high calcium snack like a yoghurt.

ALLERGENS

This is always a scary thought when starting to introduce solids. Will your baby have a reaction? What do you do if they do?

THE TOP 9 FOOD ALLERGENS ARE:

- eggs
- peanuts
- cow's milk
- tree nuts
- soy
- sesame
- wheat
- fish
- shellfish

Aim to introduce all allergen foods by 12 months, even if other family members have a food allergy. Studies show that this may reduce the chance of developing a food allergy. Introduce each food allergen individually so that if your baby has an allergic reaction you can easily identify the cause. If your baby tolerates the food, continue to offer it to your baby regularly (twice a week) which can further reduce the chance of developing an allergy.[7]

> "Only introduce one common allergy causing food at each meal, so that the problem food can be easily identified if there is an allergic reaction. If your baby has an allergic reaction, stop giving that food and seek medical advice."[7]
>
> **TRY NOT TO LET THE FEAR OF AN ALLERGY STOP YOU FROM INTRODUCING THESE FOODS.**

GAGGING AND CHOKING

A common misconception is that gagging is the same thing as choking. Gagging is a very normal part of the journey when introducing solids. Your baby will gag. A lot! It is actually a good thing! Gagging is a safety mechanism to prevent food going into the airway. In baby's the gag reflex is further forward in the mouth but take comfort knowing it does start to move further back as your baby ages. Choking is when the airways become blocked.

Some tips to prevent choking are to only offer foods of appropriate shape and texture. For example food that is finger length and width and soft enough to squash between the thumb and forefinger, particularly in the beginning. Avoid round items like whole grapes, cherry tomatoes and instead serve them quartered.

Avoiding foods because you are afraid of choking is not setting your baby up for success. Stay close, relax and let your little one explore and have fun with all of the new food that is coming their way.

PREPPING

Being organised is one way to reduce stress while introducing solids and feeding your baby. When you add more kids into the mix you'll thank yourself for taking the time to be prepared and organising. A lot of the meals in my book can be frozen. I have used Weinmeister Freezer Pods since we started our journey with Harper. Stackable and easy to use it means no food is wasted and we know we always have good nutritious meals ready to go.

Batch cooking dishes on a weekend and popping them in the freezer is great. Also prepping some finger food to pop in the fridge as well, is great.

Having snacks ready to go will not only save you time but also stop grumping kids when out and about.

THINGS TO NOTE

Before one year old there are certain things that should be avoided:
- **Honey** - it can cause Botulism as Clostridium Botulinum can be in the spores.
- **Salt** - use unsalted butter, low salt stock etc as babies' kidneys aren't able to process high levels of sodium.
- **High saturated fat foods** - just like adults these can lead to obesity and increase the risk of heart disease later in life.
- **High sugar foods** - just like in adults, high levels of refined sugars can lead to diabetes, obesity and high blood pressure.

WHY START WITH VEG?

It is best to offer vegetables first over fruit. This can help to improve the acceptance and intake of vegetables; something that we all want for our kids! Consumption of fruit is just as important as vegetables but is often more easily accepted due to a baby's innate preference for sweet foods.

From experience, I started offering fruit to Harper a lot at the start and soon realised she was rejecting any savoury flavour because of this.

As babies and toddlers become fussy it can be easy to offer fruits before vegetables which can create habits that steer them away from some key nutrients. So, ensuring our kids love veggies from day one is super important! The recommended daily serving of fruit according to Eat for Health, for a 1-2 year old is only ½ a serving - which could be half a banana, a handful of berries, a kiwi or half an apple.[8]

VEGETARIAN AND VEGAN DIETS

Vegan and vegetarian diets rely on plants as their main sources of nutrients. There are variations of vegetarians with some also eating dairy products and eggs. Vegans avoid all animal-based products. Research shows that vegetarian diets are adequate for infants and toddlers, whilst a vegan diet requires very close attention to nutrients including vitamin B12, vitamin D, calcium and protein to ensure sufficient. In infants, it is not such a concern as breastmilk or formula milk can help to deliver these nutrients.

FOOD CHOICES AND WHY

I AM PASSIONATE ABOUT FUELLING OUR LITTLE PEOPLE TO THE BEST OF OUR ABILITY BY LIMITING PROCESSED FOODS AND GIVING THEM THE BEST OPPORTUNITY TO THRIVE. BELOW ARE A COUPLE OF FOOD CHOICES THAT CAN BE CONFUSING WHEN DECIDING WHAT TO CHOOSE AND SO THIS INFORMATION MAY HELP WITH YOUR DECISION:

WATER

It is super important to note that water should only be introduced from 6 months old and should be the only other liquid in addition to breastmilk/formula. Water before one should be boiled then cooled or bottled. Juice is not recommended for babies or toddlers as it contains high amounts of sugar, isn't good for teeth and adds unnecessary calories without getting adequate nutrients, which can lead to obesity.

YOGHURT

Plain greek yoghurt with minimal added sugar. Most flavoured yoghurts will have added sugar to give them more flavour so it is best to stick to a plain/natural one.

BREAD AND RICE

Choose a grainy bread or sourdough. Low GI bread is ideal for long lasting energy. White, overly processed bread will spike blood sugar and isn't good for gut health. Same thing with rice. Brown rice has a lower glycemic index than white rice which is much better for our guts.

PRE-PACKAGED SNACKS

I know there are times when convenience is needed and pre-packaged is an easy option. I really encourage you to make your own snacks for your kiddies and opt for whole foods. Fruit, yoghurts, boiled eggs, vegetables and dip and my snack recipes, further on, are great sources of nutrients to help your little one thrive and set them up for life.

FLAPJACKS ARE THE PERFECT SNACK!
PAGE 37

PART 2: THE RECIPES

WHERE TO START - FIRST TASTES

For the first two weeks it was all about introducing some first tastes. Getting them used to having something other than milk. Around lunch time we started by offering some pureed vegetables and the corresponding finger food (or just the finger food if it wasn't puree friendly). This got them used to new flavours, different foods and introduced those savoury flavours first.

Introduce a new one every day, or so. Don't worry too much if they don't swallow a huge amount - this is just getting them used to it.

As our journey went on, these finger foods were given regularly in addition to their meal to encourage fine motor skills and keep them interested in vegetables - because let's be honest - we all want our kids to love veggies.

VEGETABLES WE DID WERE:

PUREED AND FINGER FOOD

- CARROT
- PUMPKIN
- ZUCCHINI
- BROCCOLI
- SWEET POTATO
- ASPARAGUS
- CAULIFLOWER
- POTATO

ONLY FINGER FOOD

- BEANS
- CUCUMBER
- AVOCADO (+MASHED)

PUREED VEGETABLES

FOR THE PUMPKIN, ZUCCHINI, BROCCOLI, CARROT, SWEET POTATO, CAULIFLOWER AND POTATO:

1. Chop vegetable(s) into 1-2cm pieces and steam until soft.

2. Drain the water and blend with a little milk (breast or formula) until you have consistency that can fall off the spoon.

3. Pop into freezer pods and use as needed.

TIP: AS YOUR LITTLE ONE GETS MORE USED TO TEXTURE AND FLAVOUR - PUREES CAN TURN INTO MASHED FOODS. STEAM OR ROAST, THEN MASH WITH A FORK - ADDING A SMALLER AMOUNT OF MILK (BREAST OR FORMULA) FOR A THICKER TEXTURE AND CONSISTENCY.

TIP: YOU CAN USE THESE DOWN THE TRACK TO ADD TO THINGS LIKE RICE AND PASTA OR LENTILS.

6 MONTHS +

During this stage we started with lunch and then introduced breakfast, finger foods for dinner then by seven months they were having three meals. Every baby is so different. By this stage Harper and Beau were absolutely loving purees and finger foods. Harlow wasn't interested in purees or a spoon - she would hold and nibble on finger food but overall wasn't that interested until seven months onwards. The process requires patience, consistency and exposure.

Harlow would hold her mouth completely shut at some foods. To some this would mean she didn't like it. To me it just meant she hadn't worked it out yet. Kiwi fruit and lentils were two things she just wouldn't eat. I continued to offer them to her, then at around ten months she finally picked up the kiwi fruit and ate it. YAY!

During the first couple of months, as your baby gets used to food and texture, you should be able to introduce foods with more lumps and bumps. You'll see at the start that some of the recipes are quite simple and have the option to be blended up. Then you can slowly move away from blending and on to the dishes that have more texture.

DID YOU KNOW?

AT AROUND NINE MONTHS BABIES TRANSITION FROM A PALMAR GRASP (WHOLE HAND) TO A PINCER GRASP (USING THE INDEX FINGER AND THUMB) SO YOU CAN INTRODUCE SMALLER PIECES OF FOOD.

2 SERVES

PORRIDGE

INGREDIENTS - STAGE 1

We introduced porridge with these 3 ingredients, then once they got used to it we built it up and moved to Stage 2.

- 20g rolled oats
- 120ml full cream milk
- ½ tsp cinnamon

INGREDIENTS - STAGE 2

- 20g rolled oats
- 120ml full cream milk
- 1 banana, finely sliced
- ½ tsp flax seeds
- ½ tsp cinnamon
- ½ tsp vanilla extract

ADDITION

- 1 tsp unsalted peanut butter

METHOD

1. Pop all ingredients (excluding the peanut butter) into a pot and put on a low heat. Continue stirring until cooked through and smooth - this could take 10-12 minutes. Once cooked, blend briefly with a hand blender. If adding peanut butter, add this half way through the cooking process ensuring it is mixed through.

2. As your baby gets more used to texture you will no longer need to blend it.

NOTE:
THIS RECIPE INCLUDES 2 ALLERGENS:
DAIRY AND PEANUTS.
IF THIS IS THE FIRST TIME INTRODUCING THESE ALLERGENS, ENSURE THEY'RE DONE ONE AT A TIME.

1 SERVE

SCRAMBLED EGGS ON TOAST

INGREDIENTS

- 1 egg, beaten well
- 1 slice of sourdough
  (Or grainy bread of choice.)
- Unsalted butter

METHOD

1. Heat 1 teaspoon of unsalted butter in a small fry pan then add the egg. Using a non-stick spatula, keep lifting the egg off the pan until cooked through.

2. Meanwhile, pop the bread in the toaster and lightly toast. (We don't want overly cooked toast on their little gums.)

3. Butter toast and serve eggs with a side of sliced fingers of avocado.

2 BABY SERVES OR 1 TODDLER SERVE

PANCAKES

INGREDIENTS

- 1 banana
- 1 egg
- 10g rolled oats
- ½ tsp chia seeds
- ½ tsp cinnamon
- ½ tsp vanilla extract

METHOD

1. Mash banana well then add all other ingredients and mix to combine.

2. Heat a non-stick fry pan and spoon rounds of mixture approximately 5cm in diameter into the pan. Cook for 2-3 minutes each side or until lightly browned.

3. Serve as a snack, pack them when going out and about or serve with plain greek yoghurt and berries for breaky.

Keep in the fridge in an airtight container.

4 SERVES

OVERNIGHT OATS

INGREDIENTS

- 60g rolled oats
- 150ml full cream milk
  (Or dairy alternative if dairy intolerant.)
- ½ banana
- 2 tsp chia seeds
- 50g greek yoghurt
- 1 tsp cinnamon

METHOD

1. Divide the rolled oats up into 4 containers - 15g of oats per container.

2. Pop the rest of the ingredients in a blender and blend well.

3. Divide and pour the mixture evenly over the oats and mix well. Place a lid on and store in the fridge overnight.

4. Serve as is or with some berries.

From about 18 months I added Nutra Organics Choc Whiz for a chocolaty treat. 2 teaspoons of cacao would also work.

4 SERVES

FLAPJACKS

INGREDIENTS

- 1 banana
- 40g raspberries
  (Can be replaced with blueberries.)
- 30g oats
- 40ml full cream milk
  (Or milk substitute if allergic.)
- 1 tsp peanut butter
- 1/2 tsp chia seeds
- 1 tsp shredded coconut

METHOD

1. Mash the banana well and then add the raspberries. Squish them all in, roughly. Add in all of the other ingredients and mix well.

2. Pour in a non-stick pan lined with baking paper. (It doesn't have to go to the edges.)

3. Bake in the oven at 200 degrees for about 20 minutes or until golden brown on top.

4. Cut into slices and watch your munchkin munch away.

   Store in the fridge for up to 3 days.

4 SERVES

CHICKEN AND SWEET POTATO

INGREDIENTS

- 2 chicken tenderloins
- ½ sweet potato, diced

METHOD

1. Heat an oven to 180 degrees. Wrap each tenderloin in foil and place on a baking tray to bake in the oven for 15 minutes.

2. Cover the sweet potato with water in a pot and bring to the boil. Turn down the heat and put the lid on for 10-12 minutes - until soft. (Alternatively use a steamer).

3. Puree or mash the sweet potato with a little milk of choice. Shred the chicken and stir in.

4. Using a hand held blender, briefly blend up. (As your little one gets used to texture you can stop blending so much).

4 SERVES

SWEET POTATO, LENTILS AND SALMON

INGREDIENTS

- 200g sweet potato, diced
- 1 salmon fillet
- ½ cup green lentils
- ½ tsp cinnamon
- olive oil

METHOD

1. Preheat the oven to 180 degrees.

2. Cover sweet potato with water and bring to the boil, reduce heat and cook with the lid on for 10-12 minutes or until soft. Mash or puree once cooked.

3. Place the salmon on a baking tray lined with baking paper and bake in the oven for 20 minutes.

4. While that's cooking, put the lentils in a pot with 1.5 cups of water and the cinnamon. Bring to the boil then reduce heat and simmer until all of the liquid is absorbed.

5. Mix the lentils and sweet potato together then flake through the salmon.

4 SERVES

PASTA, EGG AND PUMPKIN

INGREDIENTS

- 2 eggs
- 200g pumpkin, cut into moons
- olive oil
- nutmeg
- 100g pasta
  (I use either small shells or small penne.)

METHOD

1. Preheat the oven to 180 degrees.

2. Bring a pot of water to the boil and place room temperature eggs in for 10 minutes. Peel and set aside.

3. Cut the pumpkin and place on a baking tray with a splash of olive oil and little nutmeg. Put in the oven for 20 minutes.

4. Cook the pasta as per the instructions.

5. Drain the pasta, dice the boiled egg and mash the pumpkin with a fork. Mix it all together and serve.

2 SERVES

SALMON, PUMPKIN AND GREEK YOGHURT

INGREDIENTS

- 1 salmon fillet
- 200g pumpkin, cut into moons
- 100g greek yoghurt
- olive oil
- nutmeg

METHOD

1. Preheat the oven to 180 degrees.

2. Place the salmon and cut pumpkin onto a baking tray. Drizzle a little olive oil and a sprinkle of nutmeg on the pumpkin. Bake for 20 minutes.

3. In a bowl, mash the pumpkin with a fork, flake the salmon and then stir in the greek yoghurt until combined.

4 SERVES

SWEET POTATO DAHL

INGREDIENTS

- olive oil
- ½ onion, diced
- ½ tsp paprika
- ¼ cup green lentils
- 200g sweet potato, diced small
- 1 tsp cinnamon
- 50g baby peas, frozen

METHOD

1. Heat a pot and add a small amount of olive oil, cook the onion with paprika, until the onion is clear.

2. Add the lentils and mix. Add 1 cup of water, the sweet potato and cinnamon, making sure that the lentils and sweet potatoes are covered. Bring to the boil, then reduce heat to low and slowly simmer until the sweet potato and lentils are soft and the water has been absorbed.

3. Add peas and stir until cooked.

SALMON, QUINOA AND SWEET POTATO

4 SERVES

INGREDIENTS

- ¼ cup quinoa
- 1 salmon fillet
- 200g sweet potato, diced

METHOD

1. Preheat the oven to 180 degrees.
2. Cover quinoa with water so the water sits about an inch above the quinoa. Bring to the boil then reduce the heat and put on the lid. Simmer until all of the water has been absorbed.
3. While that's cooking, place the salmon on baking paper and pop in the oven for 15 minutes.
4. Place the sweet potato in a pot and cover with water. Bring to the boil, then reduce to low, cover and simmer for 15 minutes or until soft.
5. Drain the water from the sweet potato and mash with a fork. Add the salmon and quinoa and stir through.

6-8 SERVES

PEA, PUMPKIN AND CHICKEN RISOTTO

INGREDIENTS

- 200g pumpkin, chopped into moons
- olive oil
- nutmeg
- 4 chicken tenderloins
- 1 onion, diced
- 1 cup arborio rice
- 1 litre chicken broth or low salt stock
- ½ cup peas
- ½ cup parmesan cheese

METHOD

1. Preheat an oven to 180 degrees.

2. Place pumpkin on a baking tray. Drizzle with olive oil and nutmeg and then pop in the oven for about 15 minutes or until soft. Scrape out of skin and into a bowl – set aside.

3. Wrap the tenderloins in foil and place in the oven with the pumpkin, cook for about 15 minutes. Chop or shred into little pieces and set aside.

4. Pop some olive oil in a pot and add the onion, stirring until clear. Then add the rice and mix until combined.

5. Slowly add chicken broth little amounts at a time, continuously stirring until it's all absorbed. Repeat this process, adding broth and stirring until the rice is soft and all of the liquid has been absorbed.

6. Add the pumpkin, chicken, peas and parmesan cheese to the rice and mix until well combined.

4 SERVES

TURKEY AND ROASTED CAPSICUM BOLOGNESE

INGREDIENTS

- 1 capsicum, red
- olive oil
- 2 spring onions, chopped
- 1 tsp paprika
- 200g turkey mince
- 2 Tbsp tomato paste

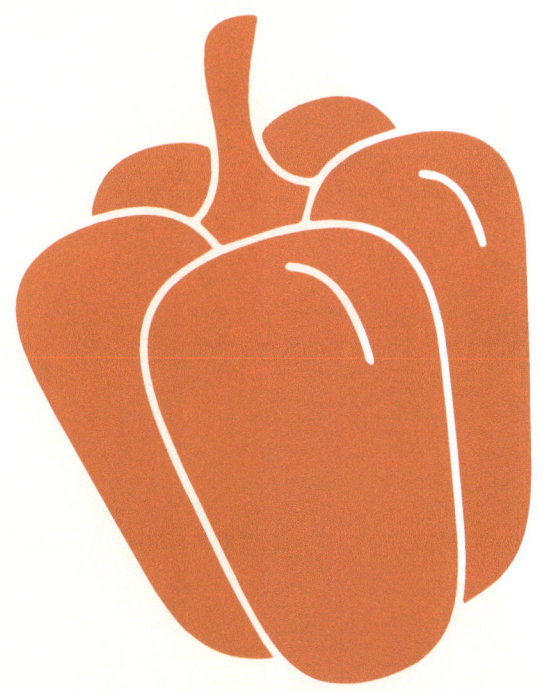

METHOD

1. Chop the capsicum in half and remove the seeds. Place it on a baking tray, skin up and then pop it under a grill for about 5 minutes until blackened.

2. Remove and peel off the skin. Dice half of it and slice the other half to save for finger food.

3. Heat a pan with a splash of olive oil. Add the spring onion and paprika until fragrant, then add mince. Break the mince up and cook until it is browned.

4. Once browned, add the tomato paste and the diced capsicum and mix well.

5. You can serve this by itself or add some brown rice or pasta.

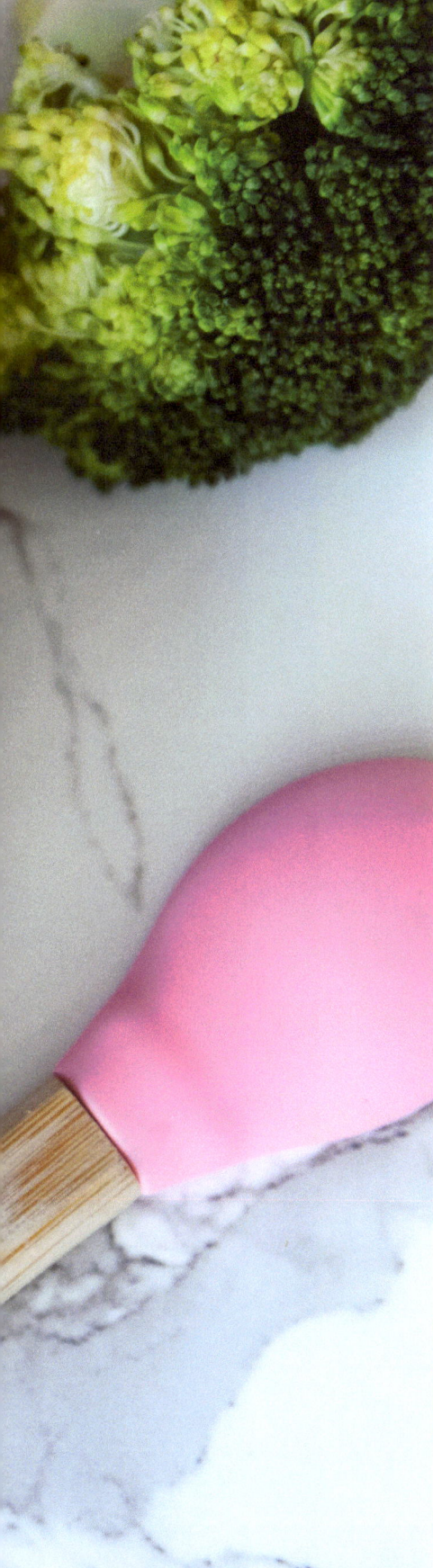

6-8 SERVES

TUNA MAC AND CHEESE

INGREDIENTS

- 250g macaroni
- 1 tsp unsalted butter
- 1 tbsp plain flour
- 1 cup full cream milk
- 1 cup cheese, grated
- 425g tinned tuna in springwater
- 200g sweet corn kernels (I use tinned)

METHOD

1. Cook the pasta as per instructions.

2. Melt the butter in a medium saucepan on medium heat. Once melted add the flour and mix until frothy. Gradually add milk, whisking as you go. (It will thicken after each addition of the milk.)

3. Once all the milk is combined turn the heat to low and stir in the grated cheese until melted. Drain the tuna and add to the sauce with the sweet corn.

4. Once the pasta is cooked - mix it through the sauce.

6-8 SERVES

SALMON AND BASIL PASTA

INGREDIENTS

- 250g penne or pasta of choice
- 400g pumpkin, cut into moons with skin on
- 1 salmon fillet
- olive oil
- nutmeg
- 100g Greek yoghurt
- handful of fresh basil, chopped

METHOD

1. Cook the pasta as per instructions.
2. Preheat the oven to 180 degrees.
3. Place the pumpkin and salmon on a baking tray lined with baking paper. Drizzle the pumpkin with olive oil and sprinkle it with nutmeg and bake for 15 minutes.
4. Once cooked, mash the pumpkin, flake the salmon and combine with the pasta, greek yoghurt and basil.

DID YOU KNOW?

... THAT A BABY'S IRON REQUIREMENT AT 7-12 MONTHS IS ALMOST 1.5 TIMES THE REQUIREMENT OF AN ADULT MAN?

8 SERVES

AVOCADO PASTA

INGREDIENTS

- 200g spiral pasta or pasta of choice
- 1 ripe avocado
- 1 garlic clove
- ½ cup baby spinach
- handful basil leaves, roughly chopped

METHOD

1. Cook pasta as per instructions.
2. Place all other ingredients into a blender and blend well.
3. Mix through pasta. As simple as that!

9 SERVES

BOLOGNESE

INGREDIENTS

- 200g small macaroni
- olive oil
- ½ onion, finely diced
- ½ cup mushrooms, finely diced
- ½ zucchini, finely diced
- ½ red capsicum, finely diced
- 1 carrot, finely diced
- cinnamon
- Nutmeg
- 250g beef mince
  (Or any mince that you'd like to use.)
- 400g tin of diced tomatoes
  (No added salt.)
- 2 tsp beef bone broth or low salt stock

METHOD

1. Cook the macaroni as per the instructions until nice and soft.
2. Add a splash of olive oil to a pan and add the onion, mushrooms, zucchini, capsicum and carrot with some cinnamon and nutmeg. Cook until the onion is soft.
3. Add the mince and cook until brown.
4. Add the diced tomatoes, bone broth and a little water if needed.
5. Turn the heat down to low and leave to simmer for up to an hour – until all the veggies are nice and soft.
6. Mix pasta and meat mixture together and serve with grated cheese.
7. You can also mix this with brown rice or use in burritos.

6-8 SERVES

CHICKEN AND MUSHROOM RISOTTO

INGREDIENTS

- 120g chicken tenderloins
- 5 mushrooms, diced
- 30g unsalted butter
- 1 small onion, diced
- 1 garlic clove, finely diced
- 1 cup arborio rice
- 1 litre low salt chicken broth or stock
- ½ cup cheddar or parmesan cheese, grated
- ½ cup spinach, chopped

METHOD

1. Preheat the oven to 180 degrees.
2. Wrap the tenderloins in foil and put in the oven for 15 minutes. Once cooked, chop or shred the chicken into little pieces and set aside.
3. Melt 5g of butter in a small fry pan and fry off the mushrooms until brown and set aside.
4. Melt the rest of the butter in a pot and add the onion and garlic until clear. Then add the rice and stir until it's covered.
5. Slowly add stock little bits at a time, continuously stirring until it has all absorbed. (Repeat this process, adding broth and stirring until rice is soft and all of the liquid has been absorbed.)
6. Stir through the mushrooms, spinach and cheese.

TOMATO ReLiSH P. 125

4 SERVES

SWEET POTATO AND SPINACH FRITTERS

INGREDIENTS

- 200g sweet potato, grated
- 1 spring onion, chopped
- 1 Tbsp fresh chives, chopped
- 20g baby spinach, roughly chopped
- 80g cheese, grated
- 1 Tbsp plain flour
- 1 tsp baking powder
- 1 egg

METHOD

1. Mix all the ingredients together until well combined.

2. Spray a fry pan with olive oil and spoon the mixture into 5cm diameter rounds. Cook until brown on both sides.

3. Serve with Brooke's tomato relish or just by themselves. Store in the fridge for up to 3 days.

9 MONTHS +

MYTH OR FACT?

"FOOD BEFORE ONE IS JUST FOR FUN."

This is actually **false.** "Food is needed for nutrition, for sensory development, for social interactions and ultimately, it's needed so that your baby can learn how to coordinate their whole body, in order to learn how to eat."[2]

6 SERVES

PRAWN FRIED RICE

INGREDIENTS

- olive oil
- ½ brown onion, finely diced
- ½ carrot, finely diced
- ¼ red capsicum
- ¼ cup frozen baby peas
- 2 mushrooms, finely diced
- 100g cooked prawns
- 1 egg, beaten
- 100g cooked brown rice
- ½ Tbsp low salt soy sauce
- ¼ Tbsp oyster sauce

METHOD

1. Heat a pan with olive oil and throw in all of the veggies. Stir fry for 5 minutes.

2. Push veggies to the side and pour in the egg, slowly lifting it from the pan, every now and then, as it cooks and scrambles. Mix the egg through the vegetables.

3. Add the cooked rice, prawns and sauce. Cook and combine for 5 minutes or until the prawns are fully heated through.

9 SERVES

SHEPHERD'S PIE

INGREDIENTS

- 1 large sweet potato, diced
- olive oil
- 1 onion, finely diced
- 1 garlic clove, finely diced
- ½ zucchini, finely diced
- ½ carrot, finely diced
- 4 mushrooms, finely diced
- 1/4 cup frozen peas
- 500g lamb mince
- 2 tsp low salt beef stock or bone broth
- 2 Tbsp tomato paste
- small bunch of fresh rosemary (Or 1 tsp of dried.)
- 1/2 cup of water
- 20g unsalted butter
- splash of full cream milk (Or milk alternative.)
- Parmesan cheese, finely grated

METHOD

1. Preheat the oven to 180 degrees.

2. Place the sweet potato in a pot and cover with water. Bring to the boil then place the lid on, turn down the heat and simmer until soft.

3. Once the potato is cooked, mash it together with the butter and milk and set aside.

4. While the potato is cooking, heat olive oil in a pan and add the onion, garlic, zucchini, carrot and mushrooms in a pan. Cook until the onion is clear. Add the lamb mince and cook until browned. Add the stock/broth, tomato paste, rosemary and ½ cup water and stir through. Turn the heat down and simmer with the lid half on for up to an hour. (You may need to add a little more water depending how long you simmer it for.)

5. Stir in the peas and mix well. Place mince mixture in a baking dish, or small single serve dishes, and spoon the potato on top.

6. Use your fork to make lines in the potato and sprinkle with parmesan cheese.

7. Place in the oven for around 20 minutes or until the top is starting to brown.

6-8 SERVES

FISH PIE

INGREDIENTS

- 3 medium carisma potatoes, peeled and diced
- 2 eggs
- 200g white fish
- 1 tsp unsalted butter
- 1 Tbsp plain flour
- 1 cup full cream milk
- 50g peas
- 1 carrot, grated
- 2 tsp milk
- handful chives, chopped
- 1 cup of cheese, grated

METHOD

1. Place potatoes in a pot covered with water. Bring to the boil, then simmer for 10-12 minutes until cooked.

2. In another pot, boil the eggs for 10 minutes. Peel and dice.

3. Put the fish on a baking tray and place in a 180 degree oven for 10-12 minutes or until cooked through.

4. While that's cooking, melt the butter in a medium saucepan then add flour and mix until frothy. Gradually add 1 cup of milk, whisking as you go. It will thicken after each addition of the milk. Once all the milk is combined turn the heat to low and stir in the grated cheese until melted.

5. Combine the eggs, peas, grated carrot and fish with the sauce and pour it into an oven safe dish.

6. Mash the potatoes using a little butter and 2tsp milk then mix through the chives.

7. Spoon the potatoes over the fish mixture and then sprinkle with cheese before placing in the oven.

8. Grill for 5-10 mins until the cheese is golden.

VEGGIE PASTA BAKE WITH (OPTIONAL) SALMON

9 SERVES

INGREDIENTS

- 2 salmon fillets (optional)
- 200g pasta – I used Oriecchette this time – but you can use penne or macaroni, your choice
- 1 Tbsp unsalted butter
- 1 Tbsp plain flour
- 300ml full cream milk
- 1.5 cups cheddar cheese, grated
- 1 carrot, grated
- 1 mushroom, finely diced
- 75g broccoli, finely chopped

METHOD

1. Preheat the oven to 180 degrees.

2. If using salmon, place the salmon on a baking tray and bake for 15 minutes, set aside.

3. Cook the pasta as per instructions, making sure it's nice and soft.

4. Put the butter in a pan over a medium heat and once melted add the flour and whisk until frothy then slowly add the milk, whisking as you go. Continue to slowly add the milk and whisking until you've used up all the milk and the sauce has thickened.

5. Take off the heat and stir in the cheese.

6. Put the drained pasta, carrot, mushrooms, broccoli and sauce into a bowl and mix well.

7. Place the mix in a baking dish and sprinkle with a little more cheese. Bake at 180 degrees for 20 minutes or until it's browned on top.

6-8 SERVES

BEEF STEW

INGREDIENTS

- 200g diced beef (Then dice it up even smaller than what they give you at the butcher.)
- ½ brown onion, diced
- 3 tsp low salt beef stock or beef bone broth
- 2 bay leaves
- 1 carrot, finely diced
- ½ sweet potato, finely diced
- 1 potato, finely diced
- nutmeg
- cinnamon
- ½ cup peas
- 2 tsp cornflour

METHOD

1. Put the beef, onion, broth and bay leaves in a pot and cover with water. Bring to the boil then turn down and simmer on low. Leave for 2 hours and make sure that the meat stays covered. (Note: You may need to top it up with water every so often.)

2. After 2 hours, add the carrot, sweet potato, potato and a dash of nutmeg and cinnamon. Leave for about an hour, stirring occasionally.

3. After the time has passed, add peas and mix in. Mix the cornflour with a little water to form a smooth paste then slowly stir it into the stew to thicken.

FRITTATA

4 SERVES

INGREDIENTS

- 5 eggs
- ½ onion, finely diced
- 1 mushroom, finely diced
- 6 cherry tomatoes, diced
- handful of baby spinach, roughly chopped
- ½ cup cheese, grated
- ¼ cup frozen baby peas
- ½ Tbsp unsalted butter

METHOD

1. Place all of the ingredients in a bowl and mix well.

2. Heat a fry pan on medium heat with some butter. Pour the mixture into the pan and let the base cook for 5-7 minutes (or until the underside is brown). Place the fry pan under a grill and grill until the top is cooked.

3. Flip the frittata out onto a chopping board, cool and chop into pieces to serve.

PUMPKIN DIP P. 91

MAKES 5

FISH CAKES

INGREDIENTS

- 200g sweet potato, diced
- 2 tsp olive oil
- 1 clove garlic, finely diced
- 1 spring onion, finely chopped
- ¼ cup parmesan cheese, grated
- 1 tsp chives, finely chopped
- 1 Tbsp greek yoghurt
- 30g plain flour
- 1 egg, beaten
- 40g breadcrumbs
- 95g tinned tuna in spring water, drained

METHOD

1. Cover the sweet potato in water and bring to the boil. Once boiling, turn the heat down and pop a lid on for 10-12 minutes.

2. While that's cooking, heat a small fry pan with 1 teaspoon of the olive oil and add the garlic and spring onion. Fry for 2 minutes.

3. Roughly mash the sweet potato with a fork and mix in the tuna, garlic mixture, parmesan, chives and greek yoghurt.

4. Mould into balls and pop on a baking tray or plate. Flatten slightly with a fork and pop them in the fridge for 10-15 minutes to cool.

5. Pop the flour, egg and breadcrumbs in separate bowls. Place the fish cakes in flour to cover, then into the egg and finally cover with breadcrumbs.

6. Heat a fry pan with the rest of the olive oil, fry the fish cakes on each side until brown and crispy.

7. Serve with pumpkin dip.

BEETROOT DIP P. 91

MAKES 8

ZUCCHINI FRITTERS

INGREDIENTS

- 1 zucchini, grated
- 1 egg
- 1 spring onion, chopped
- 1 Tbsp self raising flour
- 80g cheese, grated
- 60g sweetcorn
- 10g unsalted butter
  (Optional depending on the pan.)

METHOD

1. Mix all of the ingredients together.
2. Melt the butter in a pan, add spoonfuls of mixture to make 5cm rounds.
3. Cook both sides until brown.
4. Serve with beetroot dip.

APPLE AND DATE MUFFINS

MAKES 12

INGREDIENTS

- 1 apple, peeled and diced
- 50g dates
- 2 tsp vanilla extract
- 1 tsp cinnamon
- 1 cup rolled oats
- ½ cup self raising wholemeal flour
- ¼ cup full cream milk (Or milk of choice.)
- ¾ cup plain greek yoghurt
- 1 egg
- 2 Tbsp melted coconut oil

ICING

- 60g dates
- ¼ cup boiling water
- 30ml almond milk (Or alternative.)

TO MAKE THE ICING:

1. Blend all of the icing ingredients until paste-like consistency. Put the mixture in the fridge to cool.
2. Once the icing and muffins are both cool, place a little icing on each muffin.
3. Store in a muffin tin for up to 3 days.

METHOD

1. Preheat the oven to 160 degrees.
2. Place the apple and dates in a bowl with a teaspoon of vanilla extract and cover with boiling water. Cover and leave for 10-30 minutes (The longer you leave them, the softer they will be.)
3. While they are soaking, mix the dry ingredients in a bowl.
4. In a separate bowl, whisk the egg, milk, a teaspoon of vanilla and the melted coconut oil until light.
5. Separate apples and dates (don't throw away the water yet).
6. Blend the dates to a paste (if too thick add some of the soaking water to get desired consistency).
7. Fold yoghurt, apples and date paste into the wet mixture until well combined. Then fold the dry ingredients into the wet mixture.
8. Line a muffin tray with muffin cases and spoon the mixture in. Bake for 20 minutes until the skewer comes out clean.

MAKES 8

BROOKE'S NOURISH BALLS

INGREDIENTS

- 50g rolled oats
- 20g Nutra Organics Choc Whiz or Cocao
- 5g coconut
- 40g sultanas
- 40g dates
- 10g chia seeds
- 10g almonds
- 65g peanut butter

METHOD

1. In a food processor blitz the oats, Choc Whiz, coconut, sultanas, dates, chia seeds and almonds. Ensure it is nice and fine and the almonds are nicely crushed. (to avoid a choking hazard.)

2. Stir in the peanut butter adding a dash of water so the mixture is slightly moist.

3. Roll into balls and refrigerate for a minimum of an hour. (Unless you have children like mine who just eat them straight away!).

4. Store in an airtight container in the fridge.

TIP:

FOOD PHASES WILL COME AND GO. ONE DAY THEY MIGHT LOVE BROCCOLI, THE NEXT DAY THEY MIGHT HATE IT. JUST ROLL WITH THE PUNCHES.

TRIO OF DIPS

These are great to serve with finger foods like capsicum, cucumber and carrot, or spread them on some bread. The dips can get a little messy, but the kids will love it.

PUMPKIN DIP

- 100g pumpkin, diced
- sprinkle ground cumin
- sprinkle nutmeg
- 2 Tbsp cream cheese

Place pumpkin on a baking tray lined with baking paper and sprinkle with nutmeg and cumin. Bake at 180 degrees for 15 minutes.

Blend with cream cheese and add a little more nutmeg and cumin to taste.

HUMMUS

- 1 tin chickpeas, drained
- 1 tbsp olive oil
- ½ lemon, juiced
- 1 small garlic clove
  (Or half a large clove.)
- 1 Tbsp tahini

Blend all of the ingredients together until smooth.

BEETROOT DIP

- 1 beetroot
- 1 tbsp greek yoghurt
- ground cumin

Wrap beetroot in foil and place into a 180 degree oven for 20-30 minutes. (For ease you can also use tinned beetroot.)

Once cooked, blend with the yoghurt and cumin until smooth.

2-4 serves

AVOCADO PESTO

INGREDIENTS

- 200g tinned butter beans
- 20g pine nuts
- handful fresh basil
- ½ Tbsp olive oil
- 1 avocado, mashed

METHOD

1. Pop butter beans, pine nuts, basil and olive oil in a small food processor and blend up until desired texture. (You may want to keep more lumps and bumps as your little one gets older).

2. Mix through avocado with a spoon and serve with toast, stir through pasta or serve by itself.

PART 3: GROWING UP

As your little one develops and grows (and gains more teeth) you are able to explore with more complex flavours and textures. Once Harper got to around 18 months old, a lot of the time she just ate the same as us, which makes life so much easier. However, it is also so great to have healthy, yummy meals in the freezer ready to go when needed.

12 MONTHS+ & TODDLERS

AS WE KNOW, TODDLERS CAN GET FUSSY AND THEY LIKE TO PUSH THE BOUNDARIES. SOME TIPS THAT HAVE REALLY HELPED US OVER THE LAST COUPLE OF YEARS ARE BELOW:

1. It's important to always lead by example, if you won't eat something you can't expect your little one to. We used to play little games to make it fun. For example, "Mummy LOVES broccoli, she's going to eat yours!" It would encourage Harper to eat it all up.

2. We want to create positive relationships with food, so trying to stay calm at meal times is key. We want them to enjoy it and not have a negative association with meal times.

3. Talking to Harper about what different foods do for your body really helped her eat things that maybe she wasn't going to eat. For example, "chicken is so good for strong muscles - look at Mummy's muscles - you want nice strong muscles don't you?" "Carrots help your eyesight so you can see in the dark." "Spinach is so good for your brain so you can be super duper smart at daycare." "Rice is great for energy so you can run around lots and play with your friends."

4. Encourage them to engage their senses to help acceptance of new foods. For example, "do you think eating the carrot or cucumber will make a bigger crunch?"

5. As with babies, if Harper doesn't eat what she is given she doesn't get anything else. I never offer a different meal or treats. She goes to bed without dinner. There have been times when she's said she's hungry at bedtime and I've saved her dinner for her.

6. They don't have to eat everything on their plate but they have to give it a good go. We don't want them thinking that they always have to eat everything. They can eat until they're full. Understanding the feeling of being hungry and full are super important.

7. When introducing a new food, also offer a 'favourite' or 'accepted' food alongside the new food and only offer the new food in a small portion.

8. Fuel your little person with as much fresh, whole food as possible. As with babies, try and avoid pre packaged food that doesn't fuel them well. Low GI snacks like the ones in this book, fruit, yoghurts and boiled eggs are all great sources of nutrients.

9. Don't be afraid to let them try new flavours that you may only see as adult flavours - a little spice here and there to develop their palate.

10. Get them involved! Let them help you to make their food so that they can feel some kind of control. They will feel a sense of accomplishment knowing that they helped make it.

11. Don't hide vegetables. You want your little one to understand that vegetables are good and a normal part of their nutrition and daily meals. They may refuse some at times, just keep offering.

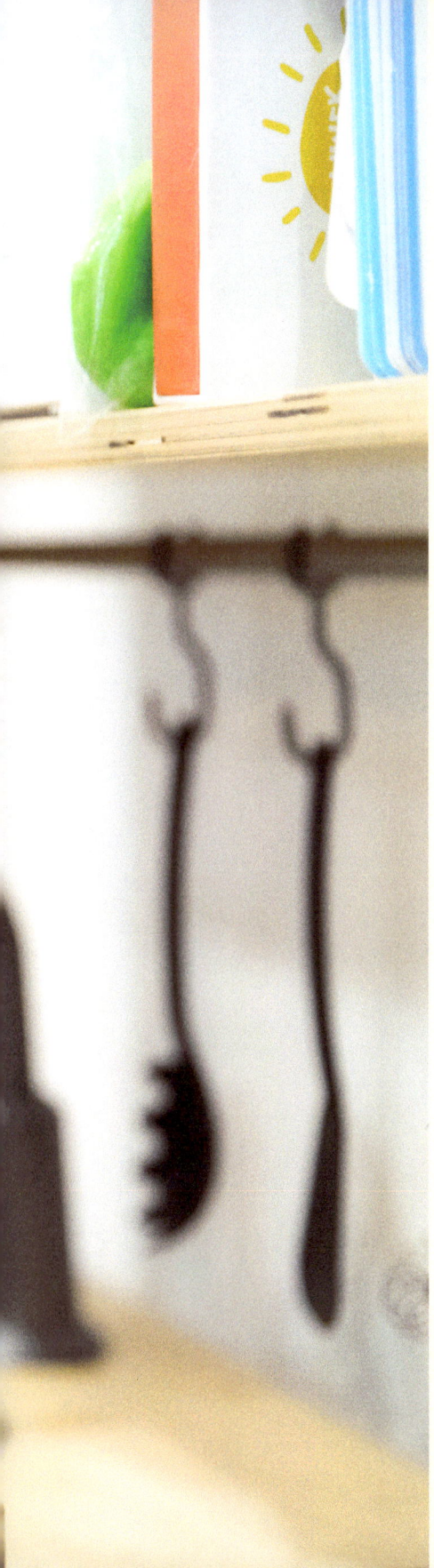

1 SERVe

SMOOTHIE

INGREDIENTS

- 200ml full cream milk (Or milk alternative.)
- 2 tsp milo (or other malt drink)
- ½ banana
- ¼ zucchini
- 2 tsp greek yoghurt
- ½ tsp chia seeds

METHOD

1. Place all of the ingredients in a blender and whiz up.

SERVES 1

EGGS AND SOLDIERS

INGREDIENTS

- 1 egg, room temperature
- ½ Tbsp white vinegar
- 1 slice of bread
- unsalted butter

METHOD

1. Bring a saucepan of water and the vinegar to a medium simmer.

2. Carefully place the eggs in the water, set a timer for 5 minutes for soft boiled eggs. (8-10 minutes for hard boiled)

3. While the eggs are cooking, toast your bread and add the butter. Slice it into rectangle soldiers.

4. Place your egg in an egg cup and using a knife tap around the edges to remove the top, dunk your soldiers and enjoy.

6 SERVES

BUTTER CHICKEN CURRY

INGREDIENTS

- 250g chicken tenderloins, finely diced
- 1/4 cup greek yoghurt
- 1/2 tsp turmeric
- 1/2 tsp garam masala
- 1/2 tsp cumin
- 1/2 tsp ginger
- 1 clove garlic, crushed
- ½ Tbsp butter
- 150g pumpkin, finely diced
- ¼ cup passata
- ¾ cup coconut milk
- 50g peas
- 72g tinned sweetcorn
- 150g cooked brown rice

METHOD

1. Place the chicken, greek yoghurt, spices and garlic in a bowl and mix well. Cover and refrigerate overnight or for a minimum of 1.5 hours.

2. Add the butter to a pan and place the seasoned chicken in, saving the remaining marinade. Cook for about 3 minutes. Add the pumpkin, passata and coconut milk then turn the heat down to a simmer for 20 minutes, until the pumpkin is soft.

3. Mix in the peas and the corn.

4. Serve with steamed brown rice.

2 SERVES

PRAWN AND SCALLOP PASTA

INGREDIENTS

- 200g pasta of choice
- 1 Tbsp Olive oil
- ½ garlic clove, chopped finely
- 2 mushrooms, diced
- 4 cooked prawns, chopped
- 2 scallops, chopped
- 8 cherry tomatoes, quartered
- handful of fresh basil, roughly chopped
- squeeze of lemon juice

METHOD

1. Cook the pasta as per instructions.
2. Pop half of the oil in a fry pan and add the garlic and mushrooms. Once the mushrooms are soft add the prawns and scallops.
3. Cook for about 3 minutes before adding the tomato and basil.
4. Stir for about 2 mins, then add the rest of the oil and stir through the pasta.

8 SERVES

CHICKEN AND SAUSAGE PAELLA

INGREDIENTS

- 2 sausages (I use country style pork style gourmet one.)
- splash of olive oil
- 4 chicken tenderloins, diced
- ½ brown onion, diced
- 2 cloves garlic, finely chopped
- ½ capsicum, finely diced
- ½ zucchini, finely diced
- 1 carrot, finely diced
- ½ tsp paprika
- ½ tsp turmeric
- 1.5 cups long grain white or brown rice
- 2 Tbsp tomato paste
- 2 Tbsp mango chutney
- 3.5 - 4 cups low salt vegetable stock or broth
- 1 tin of tomatoes
- ½ cup peas

METHOD

1. Cook the sausages on a medium heat then chop into small pieces and set aside.

2. In a large, deep pan, heat the oil and cook the chicken until brown. Add the onion, garlic, and all of the vegetables, (except the peas), paprika and turmeric and cook until the onion is soft. Once cooked, mix in the rice, tomato paste and chutney, making sure the rice is coated well. Add the stock and tinned tomatoes and bring to the boil.

3. Reduce the heat, put the lid on and cook for approximately 30 minutes or until all of the liquid is gone. (Check every now and then in case it starts to stick to the bottom.)

4. Add the peas and sausage and voila.

TOMATO RELISH P. 125

MAKES 1

DADDY'S BURRITOS

INGREDIENTS

For the mince - makes 5 serves
- olive oil
- ½ onion, finely diced
- 250g beef mince
  (Or any mince that you'd like to use.)
- ½ cup mushrooms, finely diced
- 200g tinned black beans
- 15g low salt taco mix
- ¼ cup low salt beef bone broth
- a hand of coriander, roughly chopped

For the burrito
- small wholemeal wrap
- ¼ avocado, mashed
- 1 serving of the mince
- 2 cherry tomatoes, quartered
- handful of cheese, grated
- dollop of light sour cream
- small handful of baby spinach
- 2 tsp tomato relish

METHOD

1. **Burrito mince:** Add a splash of olive oil to a pan and add the onion and mushrooms. Cook until the onion is soft.

2. Add the mince and cook until brown.

3. Add the taco mix and bone broth.

4. Add the beans (including the liquid) and the coriander and stir well.

5. Turn the heat down to low and leave to simmer for up to an hour if you wish. You may want to top with a little water to keep it moist.

1. **To make burrito:** Place the avocado on one half the wrap, layer all other ingredients on top and wrap it up.

TOMATO RELISH P. 125

MAKES 4

MINI QUICHES

INGREDIENTS

- 2 eggs
- ¼ cup milk
- ¼ cup cheese, grated
- handful of spinach, finely chopped
- 2 mushrooms, finely diced

METHOD

1. Preheat the oven to 180 degrees.
2. Grease a muffin tin with butter. Whisk the eggs and the milk. Once combined, stir in the toppings. Divide the mixture amongst the muffin cups.
3. Bake in a 180 degree oven for 25 minutes.
4. Cool and serve with tomato relish.

TOMATO RELISH P. 125
HOW TO COOK P. 128

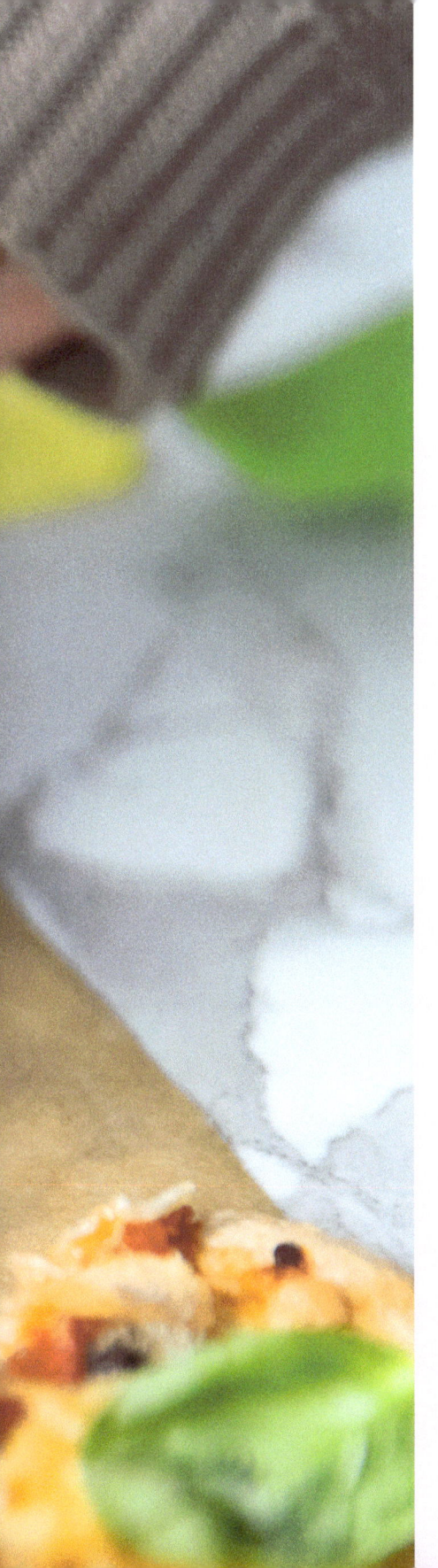

MAKES 1

PIZZAS

INGREDIENTS

- ½ Tbsp tomato relish
- 1 small wholemeal wrap
- 2 mushrooms, sliced
- 1 chicken tenderloin, cooked and shredded
- handful cheese, grated
- fresh basil

METHOD

1. Preheat the oven to 180 degrees.
2. Spread the relish over the wrap, sprinkle with cheese then scatter the mushrooms and chicken.
3. Place in the oven for 10-12 minutes. To finish, sprinkle over basil leaves.

8 SERVES

PUMPKIN GNOCCHI

INGREDIENTS

- 400g gnocchi
- 400g pumpkin, diced
- olive oil
- nutmeg
- 100g ricotta
- ½ cup parmesan cheese, grated
- 20g pine nuts
- handful baby spinach

METHOD

1. Preheat the oven to 180 degrees.
2. Cook gnocchi as per instructions.
3. Place pumpkin on a baking tray and drizzle with a little olive oil and nutmeg. Bake in the oven for 20 minutes.
4. Blend the pumpkin and stir in the ricotta and parmesan cheese.
5. Brown the pine nuts over a medium heat until golden.
6. In a pan, add the gnocchi and pumpkin mixture. Stir in the spinach and wilt, then stir through the pine nuts.

HOW TO COOK P. 129

2 SERVES

COUSCOUS PUMPKIN SALAD

INGREDIENTS

- 25g couscous
- 100g pumpkin, diced
- olive oil
- pinch of nutmeg
- pinch of cumin
- pinch of cinnamon
- ½ Tbsp red wine vinegar
- 4 cherry tomatoes, diced
- 20g sultanas

METHOD

1. Make up the couscous as per the instructions on the packet.
2. Place pumpkin on a baking tray and drizzle with a little olive oil and nutmeg. Bake in a 180 degree oven for 20 minutes.
3. Mix the spices in with the red wine vinegar.
4. Put the pumpkin, couscous, tomatoes and sultanas in a bowl and mix the dressing through.
5. Serve with a piece of steak or lamb cutlet.

4 SERVES

PUMPKIN AND SWEET POTATO SOUP

INGREDIENTS

- 500g pumpkin, diced
- ½ Tbsp olive oil
- nutmeg
- 1 onion, sliced
- 300g sweet potato, diced
- 4 cups vegetable broth or low salt stock

METHOD

1. Place pumpkin on a baking tray and drizzle with a little olive oil and nutmeg. Bake in a 180 degree oven for 20 minutes.

2. Heat a pot with the olive oil and add the onion and nutmeg. Once the onion is clear, add the sweet potato and cover with stock. Bring to the boil then reduce heat and simmer until soft.

3. Blend the pumpkin with the sweet potato mix and serve.

4 SERVES

STIR FRY WITH NOODLES

INGREDIENTS

- 250g chicken tenderloins, diced
- ½ cup broccoli, chopped into bite sized pieces
- 2-3 mushrooms, chopped
- 1 small carrot, peeled and cut into discs
- 2-3 baby corn spears, chopped in bite sized pieces
- ¼ capsicum, diced
- ¼ cup frozen peas
- 1 garlic clove, minced
- 1cm piece of ginger, minced
- half brown onion, finely diced
- 1 ½ tsp honey
- 1-2 Tbsp light sodium soy sauce
- 1ml sesame oil
- 1 pack of instant or fresh egg noodles or 1 cup of brown rice

METHOD

1. Pan fry the chicken until lightly browned and set aside.

2. Add all of the vegetables, garlic, ginger and onion and mix for 1 minute until combined, then add 2 tablespoons of water. Continue stirring for another 2 minutes and then cover for 2 minutes.

3. Remove the lid and add chicken back in. Add the sauces and continue cooking for another 3 minutes until it is all combined and the veggies are cooked.

4. Pop your noodles in boiling water to soften them then add them to the stir fry, alternatively serve with brown rice.

TOMATO RELISH P. 125

4 SERVES

CHEESE AND SPINACH ARANCINI BALLS

INGREDIENTS

- ¼ cup plain flour
- ¾ cup breadcrumbs
- 1 egg, beaten
- ½ cup arborio rice
- 1 ¼ cups vegetable broth or low salt stock
- ½ cup parmesan cheese, finely grated
- ¼ cup mozzarella, grated
- handful spinach, finely chopped
- olive oil spray

METHOD

1. Separate flour, breadcrumbs and egg into separate bowls
2. Place the rice and vegetable broth in a pot and bring to the boil, then reduce to low. Place the lid on and cook for 10-12 minutes until all of the broth has been absorbed.
3. Mix the rice, cheese and spinach together.
4. Roll into balls.
5. Coat with flour first, then egg, then breadcrumbs and place on a baking tray. Spray with a little olive oil.
6. Bake at 180 degrees for 20-25 minutes or until nice and browned.
7. Serve with tomato relish.

BROOKE'S TOMATO RELISH

INGREDIENTS

- ½ Tbsp oil
- 1 clove garlic, crushed
- 100g cherry tomatoes, diced
- ¼ cup water
- fresh basil leaves, chopped

METHOD

1. Heat the oil in a saucepan.
2. Add the garlic, stir and cook until fragrant.
3. Add the tomatoes and basil and slowly simmer.
4. After 10 minutes add ¼ cup of water then continue to simmer for 20 minutes, stirring occasionally.

HOW TO COOK

HARD BOILED EGGS

Great for a snack on the go and included in a few recipes.

I use a little white vinegar in my boiled eggs as it helps the shell to peel off easily. It's also important to place them in boiling water, not cold water and have your eggs at room temperature. If you're in a hurry - just place them under the warm tap for a couple of minutes before placing in the boiling water so the shell doesn't crack.

INGREDIENTS

- eggs
- ½ Tbsp white vinegar

METHOD

1. Bring a pot of water with the vinegar, to the boil. Add the eggs and set a timer for 10 minutes.
2. Peel straight away or leave and refrigerate for up to a week.

Poached Pears and Apples

This recipe is basically the same as my adult version, without the honey. You will also love these on your porridge, granola, yoghurt or pancakes.

Ingredients

- apples and/or pears
- cinnamon stick (Or 1 tsp of ground cinnamon.)
- ½ tsp vanilla extract

Method

1. Peel, quarter and core your fruit. Cover with water and add the cinnamon stick and vanilla extract. Cut a circle of baking paper with a hole in the middle and place over the fruit.

2. Bring to the boil then reduce to a low simmer for up to 25 minutes or until the fruit is nice and soft. Pour all of the mixture into a container saving the juice to drizzle over your breakfasts.

CHICKEN

I tend to use tenderloins in my cooking. They're a great size, soft when cooked and easier to handle. Preheat an oven to 180 degrees. Place chicken in foil and wrap it up. Place in the oven for 12-15 minutes. Feel free to add some spices to the chicken before cooking. Shred or slice the chicken and use as needed.

STEAK

I know steak can be daunting, but it's a great source of iron for growing bodies and if cooked well it is nice and soft. Over cooked steak will be tough on little jaws and teeth.

I use eye fillet, it's the lowest fat option and soft and tender. If you're at a butcher ask for it to be cut a bit thinner for your little one.

Bring a pan to a medium heat and add some spray oil, place the steak down and cook for 2-3 minutes then flip once. Leave to cook for a further 2-3 minutes on this side (depending on thickness) You only want to flip your steak once. Set aside for 2 minutes before slicing.

129

THANK YOU

This book is a long time coming. It's been sitting in my box of goals since Harper first started solids and I'm so proud it's finally here. I couldn't have made this a reality without some amazing people.

Courtney, thank you for being a collaborator on this book. I love that we share a passion for nourishing our little people.

My amazing photographer, *Michelle.* Once again you have brought a dream to life with your beautiful photographs capturing the beauty of little ones and their food.

Helena, forever grateful to have you in my life. Thank you for creating another beautiful book for me as my designer and creative muse.

Hayley, for editing this out of the kindness of your heart. Ensuring I make sense.

Brooke, without you I would still be cooking and testing some of the dishes. I couldn't have done this without you.

Bethany, the best sous chef a girl could ask for. Thanks for remaining calm as I bossed you around.

Chris, my biggest cheerleader, always supporting me and helping to test things with the kids. Thank you for being a fantastic Daddy to our little clan. Helping them along the way just as much as me so they are the healthiest little beings.

Harper, Harlow and Beau. Thank you so much for allowing your Mumma to write this book. Harper, for teaching me so much about babies and food, and allowing me to make mistakes and learn from them. Harlow and Beau also thank you for this so I didn't make the same mistakes again! You guys are the reason for this book, to help other kiddies thrive and eat as well as you.

Big love, Danni

REFERENCES

1. https://medicine.yale.edu/news-article/study-finds-snacking-is-a-major-cause-of-child-obesity/#:~:text=A%20new%20study%20has%20found,North%20Carolina%20at%20Chapel%20Hill.

2. https://childrensnutrition.co.uk/full-blog/criticalnutrients/

3. https://www.nhmrc.gov.au/about-us/publications/infant-feeding-guidelines-information-health-workers

4. https://childrensnutrition.co.uk/full-blog/criticalnutrients/

5. Eat for Health - https://www.eatforhealth.gov.au/food-essentials/five-food-groups

6. National Health and Medical Research Council, Australian Government Department of Health and Ageing. Nutrient Reference Values for Australia and New Zealand. Protein, 2006.

7. Australian Society of clinical Immunology and Allergy - How to Introduce Solid Foods to Babies for Allergy Prevention - https://www.allergy.org.au/patients/allergy-prevention/ascia-how-to-introduce-solid-foods-to-babies

8. Eat for Health - https://www.eatforhealth.gov.au/food-essentials/how-much-do-we-need-each-day/recommended-number-serves-children-adolescents-and

ABOUT THE AUTHOR, DANNI DUNCAN

Danni is a qualified and featured fitness and nutrition coach. She is mum of three; Harper and twins, Harlow and Beau. Danni has been recognised with awards in the Nutrition and Fitness space as well as a business owner. She is the author of Yummy and now Nourishing Little Lives.

Not only is Danni passionate about helping women improve their mental and physical health, but she is hugely passionate about ensuring the next generation is healthy and happy from day dot. With great relationships with food and their bodies.

Danni has seen the impact that negative associations with food from an early age can have on women later in life and is on a mission to educate people around the globe. Good health starts with nourishing and educating the smallest of our population so that they can grow up as healthy and as happy as possible. She would love to see every child thrive and love food as much as her kids!

One of my favourite things about a hard cover recipe book is that you can scribble as much as you want it in. If I look back through my favourite recipe books there are notes everywhere - from notes about the recipe, if I should double it, anything I added or took away, or any special milestones we had along our journey. So here's a space for all your scribble too.

INDEX

almond milk
  apple and date muffins 87
almonds
  brooke's nourish balls 89
apple
  apple and date muffins 87
  poached pears and apples 127
avocado
  avocado pasta 59
  avocado pesto 92

B

banana
  flapjacks 37
  overnight oats 35
  pancakes 33
  porridge 29
  smoothie 99
basil
  avocado pasta 59
  avocado pesto 92
  brooke's tomato relish 125
  pizza 113
  prawn and scallop pasta 105
  salmon and basil pasta 57
beans
  avocado pesto 92
  daddy's burritos 109
beef
  beef stew 79
beetroot
  beetroot dip 91
bread
  eggs and soldiers 101
  scrambled eggs on toast 31
breadcrumbs
  cheese and spinach arancini balls 123

  fish cakes 83
broccoli
  stir fry with noodles 121
  veggie pasta bake with salmon 77
broth
  beef stew 79
  bolognese 61
  cheese and spinach arancini balls 123
  chicken and mushroom risotto 63
  chicken and sausage paella 107
  daddy's burritos 109
  pea, pumpkin and chicken risotto 50
  pumpkin and sweet potato soup 119
  shepherd's pie 73
butter
  butter chicken curry 103
  chicken and mushroom risotto 63
  eggs and soldiers 101
  fish pie 75
  frittata 81
  scrambled eggs on toast 31
  shepherd's pie 73
  tuna mac and cheese 55
  veggie pasta bake with salmon 77
  zucchini fritters 85

C

capsicum
  bolognese 61
  chicken and sausage paella 107
  prawn fried rice 71

  stir fry with noodles 121
  turkey and roasted capsicum bolognese 53
carrot
  beef stew 79
  bolognese 61
  chicken and sausage paella 107
  fish pie 75
  prawn fried rice 71
  shepherd's pie 73
  stir fry with noodles 121
  veggie pasta bake with salmon 77
cheese
  cheese and spinach arancini balls 123
  chicken and mushroom risotto 63
  fish cakes 83
  fish pie 75
  frittata 81
  mini quiches 111
  pea, pumpkin and chicken risotto 50
  pizza 113
  pumpkin gnocchi 115
  shepherd's pie 73
  sweet potato and spinach fritters 65
  tuna mac and cheese 55
  veggie pasta bake with salmon 77
  zucchini fritters 85
chicken
  butter chicken curry 103
  chicken and mushroom risotto 63
  chicken and sausage paella 107

chicken and sweet potato 39
how to cook 128
pea, pumpkin and chicken risotto 50
pizza 113
stir fry with noodles 121

chives
fish cakes 83
fish pie 75
sweet potato and spinach fritters 65

coconut
brooke's nourish balls 89
flapjacks 37

coconut oil
apple and date muffins 87

corn
butter chicken curry 103
stir fry with noodles 121
tuna mac and cheese 55
zucchini fritters 85

couscous
couscous pumpkin salad 117

cream cheese
pumpkin dip 91

D

dates
apple and date muffins 87
brooke's nourish balls 89

E

egg
apple and date muffins 87
cheese and spinach arancini balls 123
eggs and soldiers 101
fish cakes 83
fish pie 75
frittata 81
how to cook 126
mini quiches 111
pancakes 33
pasta, egg and pumpkin 42
prawn fried rice 71
scrambled eggs on toast 31
sweet potato and spinach fritters 65
zucchini fritters 85

F

flour
apple and date muffins 87
beef stew 79
cheese and spinach arancini balls 123
fish cakes 83
fish pie 75
sweet potato and spinach fritters 65
tuna mac and cheese 55
veggie pasta bake with salmon 77
zucchini fritters 85

G

garlic
avocado pasta 59
brooke's tomato relish 125
butter chicken curry 103
chicken and mushroom risotto 63
chicken and sausage paella 107
fish cakes 83
hummus 91
prawn and scallop pasta 105
shepherd's pie 73
stir fry with noodles 121

ginger
stir fry with noodles 121

gnocchi
pumpkin gnocchi 115

H

honey
stir fry with noodles 121

L

lemon
hummus 91
prawn and scallop pasta 105

lentils
sweet potato dahl 47
sweet potato, lentils and salmon 41

M

mango chutney
chicken and sausage paella 107

milk
apple and date muffins 87
butter chicken curry 103
fish pie 75
flapjacks 37
mini quiches 111
overnight oats 35
porridge 29
shepherd's pie 73
smoothie 99
tuna mac and cheese 55
veggie pasta bake with salmon 77

mince
bolognese 61
daddy's burritos 109
shepherd's pie 73

mushrooms
  bolognese 61
  chicken and mushroom risotto 63
  daddy's burritos 109
  frittata 81
  mini quiches 111
  pizza 113
  prawn and scallop pasta 105
  prawn fried rice 71
  shepherd's pie 73
  stir fry with noodles 121
  veggie pasta bake with salmon 77

N

noodles
  stir fry with noodles 121

nuts
  avocado pesto 92
  pumpkin gnocchi 115

O

oats
  apple and date muffins 87
  brooke's nourish balls 89
  flapjacks 37
  overnight oats 35
  pancakes 33
  porridge 29

onion
  beef stew 79
  bolognese 61
  chicken and mushroom risotto 63
  chicken and sausage paella 107
  daddy's burritos 109
  fish cakes 83
  frittata 81
  pea, pumpkin and chicken risotto 50
  prawn fried rice 71
  pumpkin and sweet potato soup 119
  shepherd's pie 73
  stir fry with noodles 121
  sweet potato and spinach fritters 65
  sweet potato dahl 47
  turkey and roasted capsicum bolognese 53
  zucchini fritters 85

oyster sauce
  prawn fried rice 71

P

pasta
  avocado pasta 59
  bolognese 61
  pasta, egg and pumpkin 42
  prawn and scallop pasta 105
  salmon and basil pasta 57
  tuna mac and cheese 55
  veggie pasta bake with salmon 77

peanut butter
  brooke's nourish balls 89
  flapjacks 37
  porridge 29

pear
  poached pears and apples 127

peas
  beef stew 79
  butter chicken curry 103
  chicken and sausage paella 107
  fish pie 75
  frittata 81
  hummus 91
  pea, pumpkin and chicken risotto 50
  prawn fried rice 71
  shepherd's pie 73
  stir fry with noodles 121
  sweet potato dahl 47

poached pears and apples
  how to cook 127

potatoes
  beef stew 79
  fish pie 75

prawns
  prawn and scallop pasta 105
  prawn fried rice 71

protein powder
  brooke's nourish balls 89

pumpkin
  butter chicken curry 103
  couscous pumpkin salad 117
  pasta, egg and pumpkin 42
  pea, pumpkin and chicken risotto 50
  pumpkin and sweet potato soup 119
  pumpkin dip 91
  pumpkin gnocchi 115
  salmon and basil pasta 57
  salmon, pumpkin and greek yoghurt 45

Q

quinoa
  salmon, qquinoa and sweet potato 49

R

raspberries
  flapjacks 37

rice

butter chicken curry 103
cheese and spinach arancini balls 123
chicken and mushroom risotto 63
chicken and sausage paella 107
pea, pumpkin and chicken risotto 50
prawn fried rice 71
stir fry with noodles 121

ricotta
pumpkin gnocchi 115

S

salmon
salmon and basil pasta 57
salmon, pumpkin and greek yoghurt 45
salmon, qquinoa and sweet potato 49
sweet potato, lentils and salmon 41
veggie pasta bake with salmon 77

sausages
chicken and sausage paella 107

scallops
prawn and scallop pasta 105

seeds
brooke's nourish balls 89
flapjacks 37
overnight oats 35
pancakes 33
porridge 29
smoothie 99

sesame oil
stir fry with noodles 121

soy sauce
prawn fried rice 71
stir fry with noodles 121

spinach
avocado pasta 59
cheese and spinach arancini balls 123
chicken and mushroom risotto 63
frittata 81
mini quiches 111
pumpkin gnocchi 115
sweet potato and spinach fritters 65

steak
how to cook 129

sultanas
brooke's nourish balls 89
couscous pumpkin salad 117

sweet potato
beef stew 79
chicken and sweet potato 39
fish cakes 83
pumpkin and sweet potato soup 119
salmon, qquinoa and sweet potato 49
shepherd's pie 73
sweet potato and spinach fritters 65
sweet potato dahl 47
sweet potato, lentils and salmon 41

T

tahini
hummus 91

tomatoes
bolognese 61
brooke's tomato relish 125
chicken and sausage paella 107
couscous pumpkin salad 117
frittata 81
prawn and scallop pasta 105

tomato relish
pizza 113

tuna
fish cakes 83
tuna mac and cheese 55

turkey mince
turkey and roasted capsicum bolognese 53

W

white fish
fish pie 75

wrap
pizza 113

Y

yoghurt
apple and date muffins 87
beetroot dip 91
butter chicken curry 103
fish cakes 83
overnight oats 35
salmon and basil pasta 57
salmon, pumpkin and greek yoghurt 45
smoothie 99

Z

zucchini
bolognese 61
chicken and sausage paella 107
shepherd's pie 73
smoothie 99
zucchini fritters 85

www.ingramcontent.com/pod-product-compliance
Lightning Source LLC
Chambersburg PA
CBHW041412160426
42811CB00107B/1777